As We Forgive Those

poems by

Jessie Ptak

Finishing Line Press
Georgetown, Kentucky

As We Forgive Those

"You must face annihilation over and over again to find what is indestructible in yourself."

– Pema Chodron

Copyright © 2017 by Jessie Ptak
ISBN 978-1-63534-191-1 First Edition
All rights reserved under International and Pan-American Copyright Conventions.
No part of this book may be reproduced in any manner whatsoever without written permission from the publisher, except in the case of brief quotations embodied in critical articles and reviews.

ACKNOWLEDGMENTS

Thank you to my husband who taught me how to get quiet enough to hear my own voice. I love you.

Publisher: Leah Maines

Editor: Christen Kincaid

Cover Art: Adobe Stock OD ALL MLP Internet Order MUN TIER 1 OVERAGE, Rosemary Kracke

Author Photo: Lorraine Murphy

Cover Design: Elizabeth Maines McCleavy

Printed in the USA on acid-free paper.
Order online: www.finishinglinepress.com
           also available on amazon.com

Author inquiries and mail orders:
Finishing Line Press
P. O. Box 1626
Georgetown, Kentucky 40324
U. S. A.

Table of Contents

Folding Towels 1

Riding in Cars 2

Yellow 3

Motherhood 5

Two-Toned Palette 6

To the Woman I See Each Day 7

Other Mommy 8

Mourning the Bones 9

Earth in Mourning 10

The Difference Between Wednesday and Thursday 11

Life and Dirt 13

Misery Lane 15

The Dying Young of Pretty Things 16

Namaste 17

As We Forgive Those 19

Sacrament 20

I Don't Believe 21

Tuesday's Child 22

The Treatment Room 23

Without the Language of Birds 24

Warrior Heart 25

FOLDING TOWELS

She's heavy. Not her size, but a lot to take
in with her constant talk and bright shirts,
the thick cloud of Euphoria following
her head around the kitchen. She slams
drawers while searching for something
someone else needs. She remembers
dates, birthdays, signs up for PTA duties
eight years after her kids have graduated,
never lets her daughter go home on Monday
and Thursday nights without leftovers.
She tries her best to keep a schedule
for the highlights in her hair, covering
the gray, spending more than her husband
knows when her daughter calls in tears
that her electric's been shut off, reading
the credit card number over the phone
so her grandkids have warm bedrooms.

One night you tell her to fold the towels
herself after she peeked in the laundry
room, *you're folding them wrong.* You learn
to never talk back to a woman who's already
stretched her final inch, drawers slam, dishes
ring against glasses in the sink, words sound
bitter from her lip-lined mouth, retracting
like a spring, holding everyone together
but herself.

RIDING IN CARS

Standing on the front porch in the damp
of three in the morning, uniformed body
beside me, knock knock, stand waiting,
peeling green paint scraping the bottoms
of my toes. My father answers the door
in his underwear, glasses still on the nightstand,
questions my wakeful appearance on the wrong
side of the front door. Officer, hands on belt, tells
what he found, unlicensed boy parked his mother's
car on our road, I skipped down in bare feet to feel
something in the front seat, then the backseat, light
passing over my lids, landing on a pair of teenage
panties crumpled in the seat crevice. I rode up the driveway
in the caged backseat, cried *Please don't wake my father.*

Daddy places his face in his hands, shoulders
shaking in the dim light dripping from the skylight.
Seen him angry, seen him laugh, never seen Daddy cry, tears
landing on the tops of his legs like raccoons in the sun,
dangerous, confused. My stepping out of his pictures
hurts me more than his hands ever could.

YELLOW

Yellow is vulnerable. It's child-like,
like the color of the buttercups placed beneath
my chin in the summer when I was a kid,
like the faint shadows of their petals reflecting
off the pale of my skin. *If your chin turns yellow,
you like butter.* Yellow is as innocent
as my unclothed shoulder, fifteen-years old,
newly tanned and freckled from a June sun.

Like playing with weeds in the yard, a shoulder
like this is considered to beckon, draw
him in and say yes without saying anything
at all. It's said the victim is never the guilty;
except to groups of high school students
in a cafeteria the Monday after it all went wrong,
except to a man who says, *Well, she did it to herself.
She shouldn't have worn that.*

It wrapped to one side, bared my left shoulder,
hugged my upper body tight in its threads.
It met my denim at the hip. It gave him permission
to not ask permission. *All you have to do is say no,*
said no even after he was inside me, didn't finish
until he decided it was over, threw me on the ground,
picked me up, held me there, made me question
if I wanted it all along.

I knew him. We watched a movie, exited out
onto the pavement, didn't make it out from a bush
near the unloading dock until he took
what he wanted. That shoulder, it found
me pushed against a concrete wall, jeans
torn at the knee and wet black puddles
running through the foundation on my cheeks.

All you have to do is say no. His story was first,
I was fifteen and alone, or hanging with the wrong
crowd, or made poor judgment, or his mother should
have taught him better. *But what was she wearing?*
a dress, a shirt, a towel, a pantsuit, Superwoman's
cape. I am a woman. I put it on and it was yellow.

MOTHERHOOD

It's nothing like the books say it should be or like
what my mother told me about. It's not like the pictures
my sister in law shares of smiling and hiking.
It's not *let's go to the park or take out the paint,*
or deciding on what cake to bake.

It's not like what they said, about loving your scars,
or it's what my body can do, more like what it can't.
It's not like *you sleep, I sleep,* or fold the laundry,
wash the dishes, cook the breakfast, the lunch, the dinner
– with a smile and a nod.

It's like pulling a dark curtain
over the windows when your plans
are waiting for you to come out
and play. It's like waving *hello, goodbye,*
to sleep and food and hot cups of coffee.

TWO-TONED PALETTE

It wasn't until some time after
that baby was wrapped tight
and placed in my arms,
when I realized I was wrong,
saying I wanted someone
calling me Mommy.
It happened one morning,
hearing the ringtone
of wished-for opportunity
from between couch
cushions, a missed call,
busy with diaper tabs
and a hungry mouth,
unable to feed itself.
In this family, a woman's dreams
come in only pink or blue,
Cheerios crushed underfoot
and stale coffee forgotten
on a sticky kitchen counter.

TO THE WOMAN I SEE EACH DAY

Mom always said *Don't say that word,*
hate's a strong word, say dislike instead,
but Mom isn't here to stop the thoughts
that come to mind when I have to look
at her every day, the bulge that rises
from the bottom of the back of her faded
bra, you can see it under her shirt, hips
that carry more than they should hold.
She looks back at me with the same disgust
I have for her, says *Who are you to judge*
when I shovel a handful of fries into my docile
mouth, jumping at the knocks on the door:
Mommy, hurry, I need to pee.

OTHER MOMMY

No I want my other mommy my daughter shrieks into my face body trembling shaking finger pointing toward empty space. months of night terrors, me crawling through her door under hallway light and out of view, careful not to wake the thrashing toddler, screaming out *not my bed!*, memories we have no recollection of, just watching in the night until she settles, settles, down into a deeper sleep. finding out her other mother keeps her entertained at her little green table while her sister screams for me, other mommy wears dresses, and she tells me *mommy I want to wear more dresses,* she starts speaking in a foreign tongue, *my other mommy talks like this.*

MOURNING THE BONES

Shots ring out, blow through
the high grasses hours before daylight,
leaving your mother to thump in the dust
of the ground below your heavy feet.

At the side of her body, the herd gathers
around, listens to your cries, watches
as you lift your trunk, grazing cold
and wrinkled skin, tears leaving empty

tracks through the dirt below your eyes.
You nudge her under her front legs, step
on her ears, waiting to see an eye open,
a twitch of her tail. Four days later

you'll leave her side, men will come and take
what isn't theirs. The body will dry in the Africa
heat, animals will feast on the remains
of the dead. You pass the mound of bones,

run your snout against the curve of the skull,
offering twigs and leaves for burial. A foot
digs into the earth as you bow your head
with sunken eyes, falling silent beneath the sun.

EARTH IN MOURNING

The Earth cries,
shrinks away from the heavy
gray above. Wind swirls against
the coming winter stillness,
speaks a silence through the branches.
Birds move quick in patterns,
synchronized to seconds.
The Earth cries.
Lights stutter across the sea,
dimming, fading, turning
down for the night, city of lights
gone dark. A candle ignites.
The Earth cries,
shoulders shuddering
with the weight
of man's carnage.
The Earth cries,
depleted to the verge
of collapse.
The lights are off, but one
sparks a candle, two, then two
more. The candles are burning
and the Earth cries.
Seas still as the sky, the flames
are quiet, gathering, flickering
humanity, more love.
The Earth cries for more love.

THE DIFFERENCE BETWEEN WEDNESDAY AND THURSDAY

I'd rather be home, but woke up
with tubes running from my lungs
to clear cases filled with fluid; need help
walking to the bathroom, Room 608.

On a Wednesday I went to bed
a forty-three year old man,
Thursday went to bed with a chemo
appointment, stage four, a list
of words that never passed through
my throat the day before they found
an esophageal tumor.

People always come to tell stories,
to laugh, to cry, to say *how ya doin'
bud?* One rubs my feet, one places
a photo of Christ at the foot of my bed,
under a TV playing Christmas cartoons.

My niece made a cheesecake I can't eat;
the cancer won't let me swallow.
Homemade cheesecake is better
than cheesecake on a rolling cart.
She made it from scratch.

My daughter comes in, sits at my feet,
tears soaking her face, twenty-years
old, wearing a twenty-one tiara, pink fluff
and glitter. Her birthday is in June, Father's
Day. We're celebrating early.

My sister says goodnight, rests her head
on my caved-in chest that once bellowed
out, my heart still beating for now.
She lifts her head, turns for the door,
my hand pulls her back, eyes lock,
mouths closed. *What the fuck.*

When you find out you have three
weeks left to live on Thanksgiving,
you suddenly wonder
what it is you thanked
God for last year.

LIFE AND DIRT

It's Fall and the dirt cracks
easy under Daddy's steel
shovel, pointing to the earth
then breaking it, pointing, breaking,
until the small box gently folds
into the earth's skin. A heavy-sided
box, paper-made, not wood,
just enough space for a curled up
cat to lay, orange matted hair
against its open wounds and flesh,
eyes still open after seeing the front
of the after-school bus.

Placing him gently in, standing
for a moment, under the leafless
tree, early November. I rush inside
to finish my homework.

It's Winter and the dirt is solid
cold with jutting rocks.
The cancer marches through
my uncle's veins and takes the living
out of him before the last date
on his shiny new rock.
I sit in a corner in my grandmother's
home, his soul leaves the dust
and particles, gives way to rays of sun
from gathered clouds above the fields
behind the backyard.

My heels stick to the surface, toes numb
from the air. It's just a box, shining
and mahogany, roses placed on top. It creaks
and groans into the ground. I stand
with others draped in suffering, look up
to his rainbow, mid-December, across gray
clouded sky. I smile, unapologetic
for the tears I haven't shed.

MISERY LANE

Lay me out on the asphalt, trails of smoke
and cold blood on my matted head, charred
lips and eyelids, face black and bitter like the dark
of the March night. Lay me in the street alongside
the girls who stood hunched over sewing needles
in the Asch Building hours before turning to ashes.
Lay us up and down the water's edge.

Sixteen diamonds lay scattered in the coals,
one solitary emerald, small enough to fit
the finger on my hand, to give this blackened
body a name, a story. Mother will stop running
ivory thread through the celebratory dress.
The man I love will toss a rose on cold dirt;
he will find someone new to wear an emerald
ring and I will lie with nameless sisters
beneath the Brooklyn ground.

THE DYING YOUNG OF PRETTY THINGS

Both feet in a puddle
in the parking lot of a church,
nearing midnight and I wonder
if the embrace of the stinging rain
on my bare arms could be your long
fingers closing in on my skin.

Inside, your mother covers her ears
as an ambulance rushes outside,
sirens blaring and echoing through
the empty sanctuary, tending
to a driver's wet pavement mishap,
holding the body as it did yours.

You're buried across the street when
the sun comes out and warms the dirt,
breaking easy under shovels. I wear pink,
not black, the color of your lips, your soul,
the color of the flat shoes that twisted
with your legs under your school desk.

I drop a pink rose into the open earth,
make my way through tall hot grass,
think of your yellow windbreaker
and how it always smelled of vanilla
and softener, how you liked pretty things,
full and dainty, budding elegance.

Sometimes when the sun sets over the ridge
behind our high school, where we learned
to grow and to stay young, the clouds swipe
and brush across the sky, pink hangs near
the horizon, glinting through the wisps
of white and I think – I know – *there you are.*

NAMASTE

I tried to avoid him as he turned toward me,
his black pocketed jacket zipped halfway,
thick gray cords of mopped hair smothering
his scalp, reaching down toward his face.
I was reading alone at my favorite table
in my small town's cafe when his blue eyes
looked out to the rain and he found a table
next to me, said *happiness can't depend
on outside circumstances.* I didn't ask
him to tell me about surviving misfortunes,
about his ex wife's mother, father, molestation
when she was a child; he chose to marry
her because of the pain he wanted to mend,
how he thought he was gay after the priest
grabbed his balls when he was twelve. He said
beauty surrounds him, he's grateful to be human,
kindness to all, that a quicker fix than prison
is a swift bullet to the brain, child molesters
are for life. *Sometimes a teenaged girl is cute
but you don't cross that line.*

How lovely life is, the bliss in a rainy day,
he told me of his nephew's schizophrenia,
there's no middle ground between numbing
medication and staring at your hands, accusing
your parents of changing them overnight
while you were sleeping. He stopped to ponder,
sighed, thanked God for giving him a sun in hell.
Unzipped his black jacket, pulled out a clear
bottle, poured a healthy dose of vodka into fresh
apple juice, local old men looking away, out

to the street. *I'm here on a spiritual retreat, Blue Cliff Monastery*, raising his hands in prayer above his heart, *namaste*. A thud on the floor exposed a brown bagged beer can saved for later before he shrugged and tucked it back into a pocket in his black nylon jacket.

He parted from his seat, the bitter sharp scent of spirits flooded across my table, told me how grateful he was to speak with me about Universal Laws and the vehicle he calls Martin, adorned with male organs he said are in use from time to time, now and again.
Hands to the heart, *Namaste*, walked out the door, stood near the front window to smoke a cigarette, shaking hands reaching into his black jacket for a second bottle of burning retreat.

AS WE FORGIVE THOSE

Ephesians 6:1-4 *Children, obey your parents in the Lord, for this is right.* Talk stories with Dad, grandpa, grandma, he leans far back in his chair, narrowing eyes, a hard shell of anger between the Dad we know and a father we don't. The mother, *grandma*, wanted the world and that's what she got while all six kids were at home with a new sitter a week. Money flowing in and babies popping out, *And God said to them, be fruitful and multiply*, too busy with each other to know Two's favorite snack, if Five took her first steps, dad was Four, Fours get ignored. Babies by number, hesitant to give too much love, but quick to teach of a God to be feared, kids punished for running or making noise or maybe just being in the wrong room at the right time, *Proverbs 13:24 Those who love their children care enough to discipline them.* Twenty-seven years of watching as Dad took turns tugging the ropes of love and resentment, his parents standing between, *Proverbs 20:20 If one curses his father or his mother, his lamp will be put out in utter darkness.* He always told me he'd love me no matter my choices, never mentioned the Bible or going to church. *Dads only give us what they can with what they've been given themselves.* I sit across from him at the diner, flattening out the white paper wrapper of my straw, looks up from his chicken salad, *Now let me ask you, do you pray?* Think of them, the grandparents and the rosary, the God they feared, same God he fears, a God I don't know, don't claim, *Psalms 103:13 As a father shows compassion to his children, so the Lord shows compassion to those who fear him,* the abuse of my father's heart, his boy skin bruised and healed into an armor of man, look up and smile, *Something like that.*

SACRAMENT

They weave the white
ribbon through the thick
of your crow hair, slip it in curls,
pat your crown and tug
your skirts of lace taut and long.
I'll tell you a secret, little sister:
Christ isn't in a tall box of wood,
a tomb of gray stones and granite,
that shining cage, baited with promises
of promised lands, of redemption,
free. Who's to play the role of God,
draped in robes and gold?
Better to look past stained
glass, to babbling water in the backyard
creek. *Come with me,* where hope
lives, where beginnings
come after ends. *Take my hand,*
leave your ribbons in the street.

I DON'T BELIEVE

> *"Every night I ask the Lord, 'Why?' and haven't heard a decent answer yet."*
> - Jack Kerouac, Desolation Angels

Maybe it's because I've decided I don't believe
in a God or a gated-community-type heaven,

why God won't answer, or is it because my husband
accuses me of jumping in to steal the last word,

talking too long and too loudly to hear a response.
Though I don't believe there's an answer enough

to why a fleshy-faced baby under a minute
old would be chosen to house a single-sided

heart, too weak to pump blood for a growing
body, too beautiful for us to consider a burial

site, flipping through shiny catalog pages for a perfect
shirt-sized wooden box made for holding a little body.

I hear the last breath, and I've heard he listens.
I ask again, but maybe even God is short on answers.

TUESDAY'S CHILD

I'm sure she wandered a light-filled
hallway of glass, scanning faces to find
kind eyes, the smile of her mother,
strong hands of her father. She sat
in a room of bright white with Source
to go over the fine print of a renewed
contract, leaving to live another life,
to learn lessons on the human plane.
Fine print said this would not be easy,
scalpels drawing straight lines
down the center of her fleshy
chest, Mom she hasn't met yet
crying in the hospital elevator, lights
shining down from bulbs placed overhead
to see into the tunnels of the cavity
of her heart. Bringing to agreement
life lived wrapped in wires and the bitter
antiseptic scent flooding from green
wrappers, waiting on injections, thinning
blood to stay for another tomorrow,
living for the purpose of showing others
how to live.

Born on a Tuesday, third day of the week,
under guidance of Mars, the will to win,
perseverance, progression, even if the heart
comes in half the normal size or if the arteries
constrict too tightly.

THE TREATMENT ROOM

The Child Life Specialist comes to our room and says *It's time,* do I want to go or stay here in front of the window that sees the city? I stay on the pulled-out plastic cot, covered in sanitized sheets, handing my baby to the dark-haired girl, younger than my twenty-six-year-old self. I add a rattled green butterfly to my daughter's belly, something that smells like me, something she knows.

I close the door behind them, muffling noises traveling from across the hall, knowing she's laying on the covered cold metal table, white lights overhead and the stinging tang of antiseptic alcohol swabs, swabbing the empty skin inside her elbow. This is where babies cry at the purple rubber bands tied to their only free parts, pulling taunt at their healing skins and fleshy outsides, where babies who talk cry for mommies and daddies–or just someone else's normal.

They bring her back. She bobs her brown haired head and sucks the sugar water off a green BPA-free pacifier, sees me, strikes a fight against me with her eyes.

WITHOUT THE LANGUAGE OF BIRDS

I watch you in your sweatshirt, drinking coffee,
staring past the Boston Globe, away
from passers-by. I see a man sitting next
to you, suit and tie, picking apart a croissant.
As a mother with a yellow plastic pass
around my neck, it comes natural to ask,
Is your child dying here?

Do fathers of dying children wear
striped button-downs on otherwise
ordinary Tuesday mornings, when the sun
reflects off the Eastern glass of the city?

Do fathers of dying children wear
old college t-shirts, with lines beneath
their bottom lashes, with flattened hair
from plastic pillows on pull-out cots?

There's something to be said about new light
glinting between high-rises, bouncing
from the Charles. Business people will fill
the night's empty spaces in the parking
garage, spaces between the night-time cars,
plates from other places, our cars sitting
still from the moment we arrive, days,
sometimes weeks before. Day visitors
file in and out, more sick kids in the lobby,
masking their germs,
riding in chairs,
lugging their tanks.

When you watch the day wake in the still
of this lobby, the truth of the night has nowhere
to hide. Little eyes close, machines still sound,
like bluebirds from the chilled window of a daughter's
intensive care unit room, nesting in the gardens.
They chat amongst themselves in the rising daybreak,
speaking of things unknown without the language of birds.

WARRIOR HEART

i.
*Blood pumps out over here and back
in from the lungs through here,* marks
paper with a pen with eight colors
of ink, arrows pointing left and right,
two diagrams of a heart, one normal,
one missing one side; underdeveloped
left ventricle, unopened mitral valve,
narrowed aortic arch. Hypoplastic
Left Heart Syndrome: *Let me know
what you're doing, two more weeks
if you want to abort.* Waiting
for the elevator, my husband reaches
out to scoop me up before I hit the floor,
hands cupping my elbows.

ii.
I sit on our bathroom floor, yellow tiles
on the wall, three hours between feedings,
writing down the daily weight, calories
consumed. She can't be touched underneath
her arms, sternum wired shut after
it was cracked open, blood rewired, hairlike
veins and pathways crossing, heart
the size of a walnut. The right ventricle
works a job meant for two, a manmade
shunt between pulmonary arteries
and aorta, forcing blood to the lungs.
I cry on the bathroom floor, same clothes
as yesterday, afraid of my blue baby,
of her breathing, the chance of dying.
Who am I to be given something so fragile,
on the edge of death?

iii.
Recovering from the trip to the cath-lab,
a balloon inflated and replaced by a stent
to clear a clot in the pulmonary artery,
after a nine percent blood flow to the left
lung. My husband left to go home to another state,
the draft coming in through the window, a view
of Fenway. The baby's eyes stay closed, her chest
and belly rise and fall, taking monitor stickers,
green and black wires with them, light of the screen
showing safe numbers, turning her skin bright blue.
I cried when the nurse showed me the angle
for shooting an injection of blood thinning juice.
Baby smiled at me ten minutes after the pain
left her leg, laughed at the turtle hanging above
her head, swayed her chubby face to the music.
I cranked that mobile for three hours straight,
no food, no sleep, just to see her smile and giggle
four days after major surgery, to learn the struggle
of heroic love, to learn the ways of a warrior heart.

www.ingramcontent.com/pod-product-compliance
Lightning Source LLC
LaVergne TN
LVHW041518070426
835507LV00012B/1671